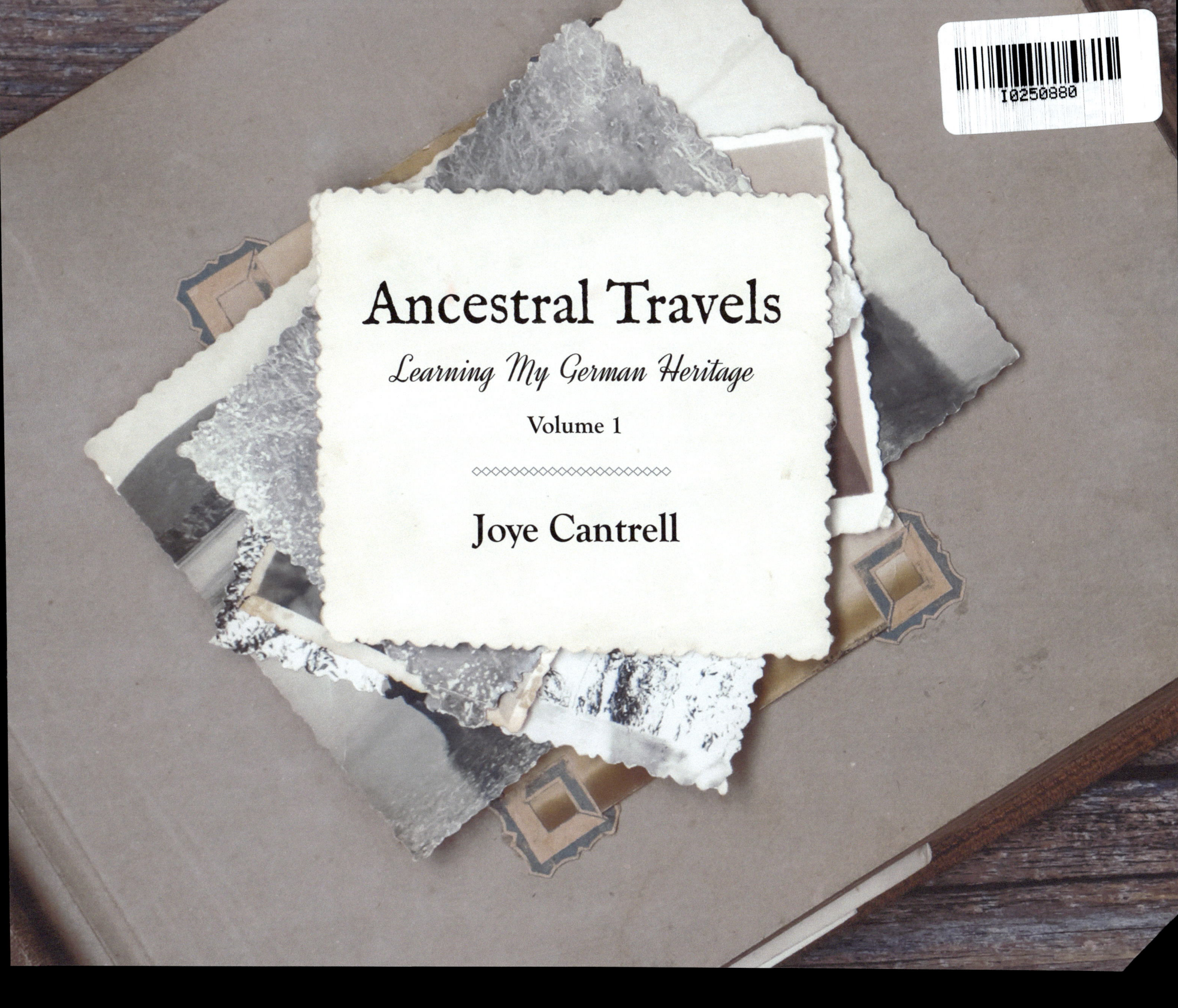

Ancestral Travels
Learning My German Heritage
Volume 1
Joye Cantrell
Published April 2024
Heirloom Editions
Imprint of Jan-Carol Publishing, Inc.
Illustrations were created using acrylics, pencil, and ink.
Photographs: photo album © Avalepsap/Adobe Stock
Book design by Tara Sizemore

This book may not be reproduced in whole or part, in any manner whatsoever, without written permission, with the exception of brief quotations within book reviews or articles.

Copyright © Joye Cantrell
ISBN: 978-1-962561-26-6
Library of Congress Control Number: 2024939857

You may contact the publisher:
Jan-Carol Publishing, Inc.
PO Box 701
Johnson City, TN 37605
publisher@jancarolpublishing.com
www.jancarolpublishing.com

In Memory of My Mom

Charlotte Brooks

1933–2023

This book is dedicated to all the family genealogists who have worked long hours of research on their family archives, catalogued family photos and memorabilia, conducted internet searches on lost connections, and generously shared with family members, even the skeletons in the closet, like me.

"Finding the path our ancestors walked is not always easy, but the rewards of the journey make the effort worthwhile."

— Jayne McGarvey

Table of Contents

Preface..1

The Genealogist..3

The Geb and Gest of the Graveyard...4

Westphalian Emigrants..7

Ladbergen of the Past..8

Tenant Farmers..11

Provider and Protector...12

Homemaker and Caregiver..15

Children's Chores and Household Tales...16

A Prosperous Cottage Industry...19

Beekeeping..20

Protecting the Flock..23

Military Service..24

Work in the Peat Bogs..27

Faith and the Church..28

Moving Day..31

Across the Big Pond...32

Apfelpfannkuchen or Pfannkuchen..35

About the Author..36

Bibliography...37

Preface

This book was inspired by the weekly Zoom meets that my German cousins, several times removed, arranged during the quarantine days of the Covid-19 Pandemic. There is always intriguing chatter about our German ancestors during these meetings. Ship logs, old photos, or a family recipe might be shared. Much of the information is kept in a well-organized file cabinet. But I longed for more. This book attempts to revisit what life might have been like for our relatives from historic Westphalia, Germany. It hopes to answer the common questions of how did they make their living? What were their daily chores like? What did they eat? Why did they move from a home that generations of Aufderhaars had lived at to travel across the ocean to start a new life? It also examines some of the personal traits and qualities that have at times come to define us. These are generalizations drawn from my family and from researching my German ancestors.

My research comes from past historians, reenactors, cookbook authors, and family genealogists. I have attempted to illustrate my ancestral travels using acrylics in the impressionistic style. I hope this book inspires others to conduct their own ancestral travels and to appreciate their heritage.

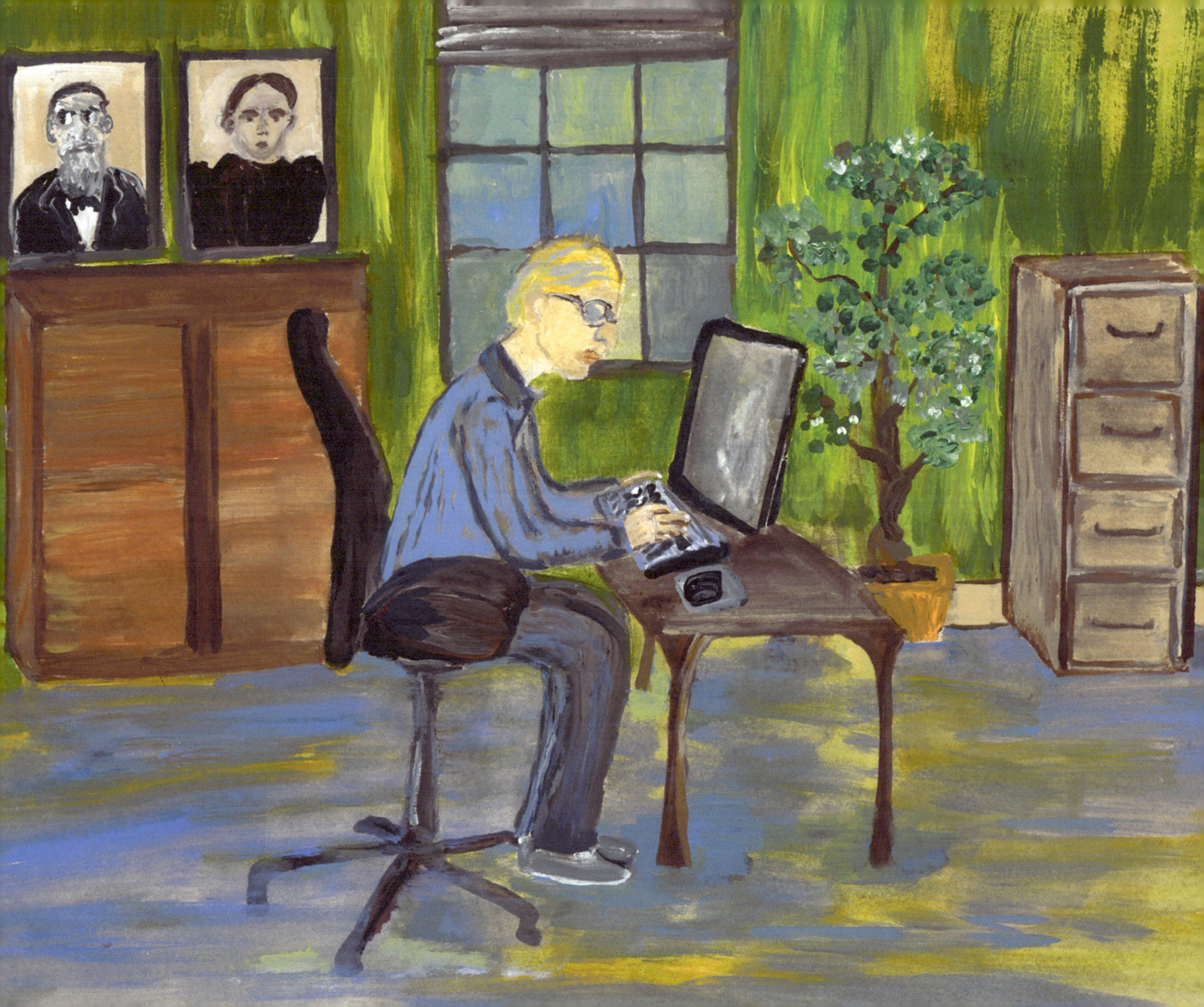

The Genealogist

*"A concerted effort to preserve our heritage is a vital link to our cultural,
educational, aesthetic, inspirational, and economic legacies —
all of the things that quite literally make us who we are."*
— Steve Berry

Life in the file cabinet is always developing as family researchers continue to contribute to the archives. All this information needs to be carefully inventoried, cataloged, and filed. Without the archivist, our connections to our ancestors, our understanding of our personal heritage, and our traditions could easily become lost. Their work is invaluable.

Our family records are rich in information, images, and stories, but there are still some mysteries that are waiting to be revealed. My side of the family was one of those discoveries. We had been hidden due to a family scandal that was hushed up. Such revelations can cause quite a stir and can cause members to question their past impressions of their ancestors. The choices of our ancestors have long-lasting, multigenerational effects. My distant cousin had learned of our existence through a letter from my mother to her biological mother. It was a quest that had been sadly denied. I did not learn of my grandmother's existence until I was well into adulthood.

It is a constant quest to discover these lost narratives. Our research has come from genealogical online databases, government records, family interviews, old letters, photos, diaries, family Bibles, and personal travels to our ancestral homes. More recently, DNA tests are being used to unlock our genetic blueprints. They may certify or disavow the validity of those family stories.

With more research, more questions are generated. What were their lives like in faraway Germany? Do I possess certain skills, inclinations, or abilities that were distantly passed down to me? And why did they come to America?

The Geb and Gest of the Graveyard

"The only real equality is in the cemetery."
— German proverb

The quest to know my ancestors would commence with a journey to Missouri for a family reunion at the cemetery. This was the ideal location to meet my lost relatives, both living and dead. For some, visiting graveyards seems macabre. As a tombstone tourist, I have always found them informative, peaceful, and architecturally intriguing. Epitaphs can be powerful statements of a family's love for the deceased, a reference to their career, or a testament of their faith. You wonder what life was lived between the dates. Paying respects to past relatives can lead to deep introspection.

Initial meetings with new family can sometimes be awkward. My distant cousins made that first encounter most welcoming and comforting. Being accepted by those related to you is a gift and a blessing. I felt valued and blessed to discover these new connections that were willing to share their histories and traditions. They were very eager to learn about a new Sturm/Auf-der-Haar descendant, and I was pleased to oblige.

They lead me to my grandmother's grave. It was comforting to see her final resting place, but sad to know that my mother had been forbidden to know her. You yearn to discover your biological roots, but there is also a fear of being rejected.

We walked on to see the graves of our Great Great Grandparents. Heinrich Aufderhaar was born in 1832, in Ladbergen, Westphalia. His wife, Mary Elizabeth Auf-der-Haar, was born in 1845 in Holstein, Missouri. It was Mary's parents who had traveled from Ladbergen in 1841. What memories did they share of their homeland? What was their life like between their geb (birth) and their gest (death)? It was time to take an ancestral travel of my own to strive to answer these queries.

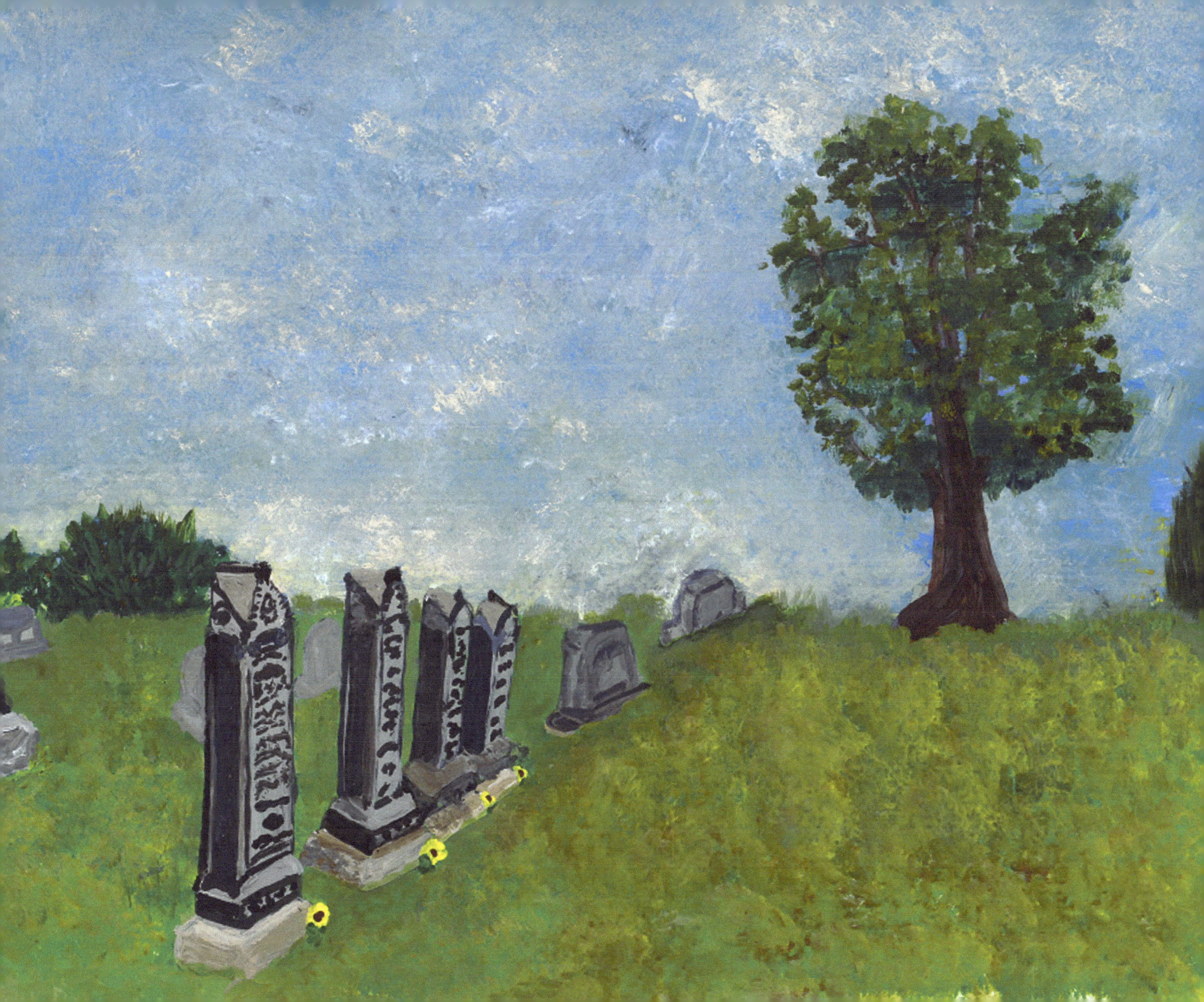

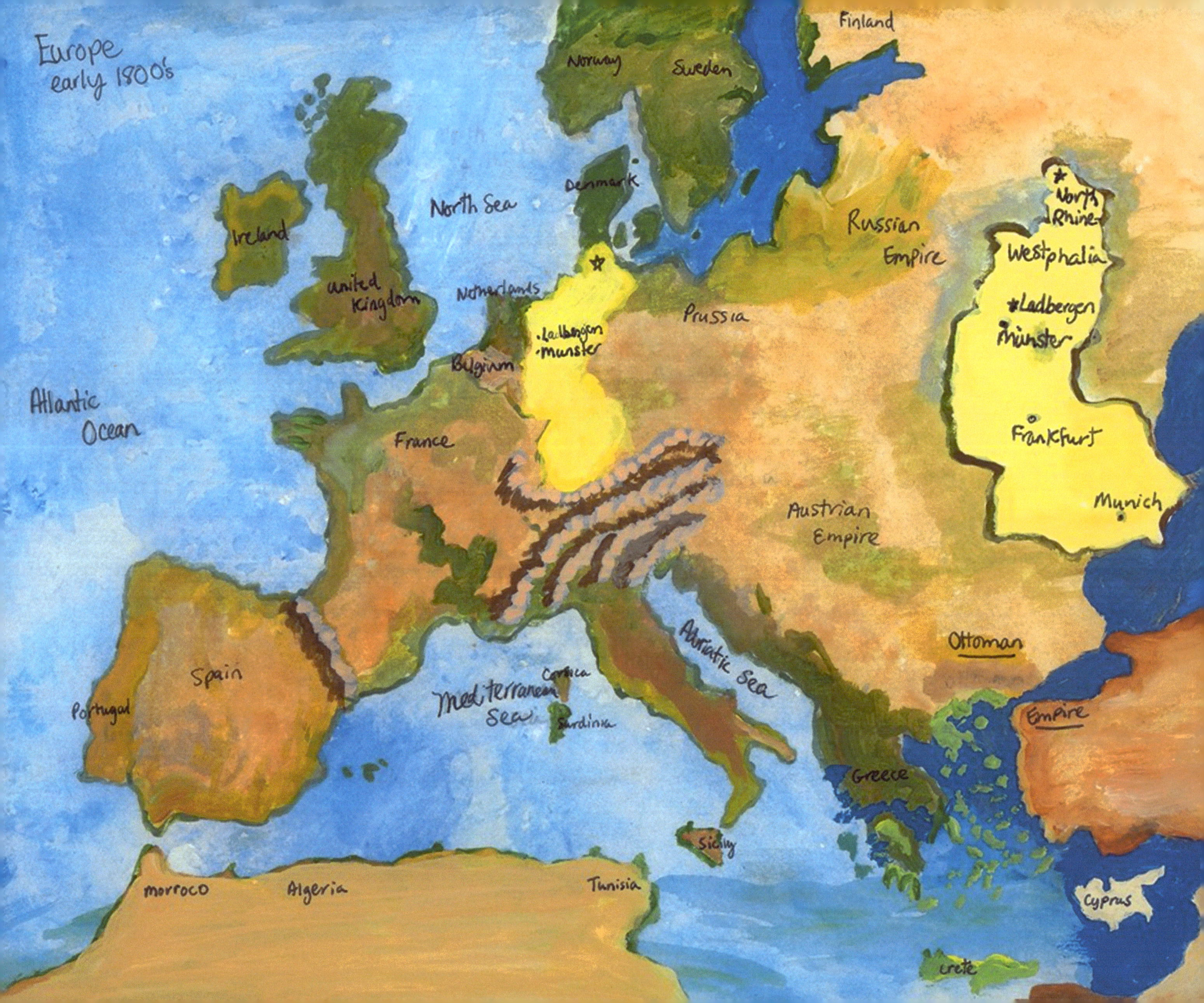
Europe
early 1800's
Finland
Norway
Sweden
Ireland
United Kingdom
North Sea
Denmark
Netherlands
Ladbergen
Munster
Belgium
Russian Empire
Prussia
North Rhine-Westphalia
Ladbergen
Münster
Frankfurt
Munich
Atlantic Ocean
France
Austrian Empire
Spain
Portugal
Corsica
Mediterranean Sea
Sardinia
Adriatic Sea
Ottoman Empire
Greece
Sicily
Morroco
Algeria
Tunisia
Cyprus
Crete

Westphalian Emigration

"The most dangerous worldviews are the worldviews of those who have never viewed the world."
— Alexander von Humboldt

The historic Westphalia was located southwest of Denmark and east of the Netherlands. It was a province in Prussia. Germany did not become a unified country until 1871. Our small town of Ladbergen was northeast of Munster.

Our ancestors were amongst the million that would eventually migrate to America during the 1800s. About 40% of the population of Ladbergen emigrated during the 19th century. This was the highest emigration rate in Germany during that period. They departed mainly due to economic hardships and so they moved for the promise of work. Farms were becoming less fertile and affordable chemical fertilizers were still in the distant future.

The possibility of owning your own farm was also limited due to inheritance laws and taxes. Most were tenant farmers, working properties that were too small to make a sustainable living. With escalating population growth and fewer sources of income, poverty and crime had also increased. Prospects for living a comfortable life in their current home had become doubtful.

Ladbergen of the Past

"People will not look forward to posterity who never look backward to their ancestors."
– EDMUND BURKE, REFLECTIONS ON THE REVOLUTION IN FRANCE

Attempting to visit the homeland of your ancestors is not always a possibility. Through others' research, it became apparent that the home of our ancestors, the Aufderhaars and Auf-der-Haars, no longer exists. The heaths, marshland, massive sand dunes, and extensive farmlands are gone to housing developments, industry, shops, and roads. During World War II, Ladbergen was heavily bombed due to its canals. I would therefore need to rely on written accounts, old photos, and my imagination to experience my ancestral homeland.

According to the family research, our Auf-der-Haar, Aufderhaar, and Feigenbaum ancestors were from Ladbergen. Family names were often recycled to keep the memories and legacies of relatives close and distant alive. Names were sometimes changed upon coming to the United States. Middle names could become first names, and German-sounding names like Heinrich could be Anglicized to Henry. Many immigrants chose to change or simplify their names after citizenship.

Johann Heinrich Wilhelm was listed as Herrmann Auf-der-Haar, a farmer on the passenger list of the Leontine, which departed from Bremen in 1841 for Baltimore, Maryland. He was 32 years old, and his wife, Christina Ann Elisabeth Feigenbaum, was 29. They had three children: Wilhelm, 8; Elisabeth, 4; and Christine, 1½ years old. Their in-laws sailed with them. Johann Hermann Heinrich, listed as Herman Feigenbaum, was 50 and a carpenter. His wife, Elisabeth, was also 50. Their two children came with them. Herman Heinrich was 18, and his sister, Christine Feigenbaum, was 21. There were 56 Ladbergen residents that were on the ship. Occupations included shoemakers, weavers, farmers, and carpenters.

I imagined my distant relatives being tenant farmers on a small plot of land of maybe 3–5 acres. A small cottage in a field of summer flax with nearby oak trees and juniper shrubs first came to mind.

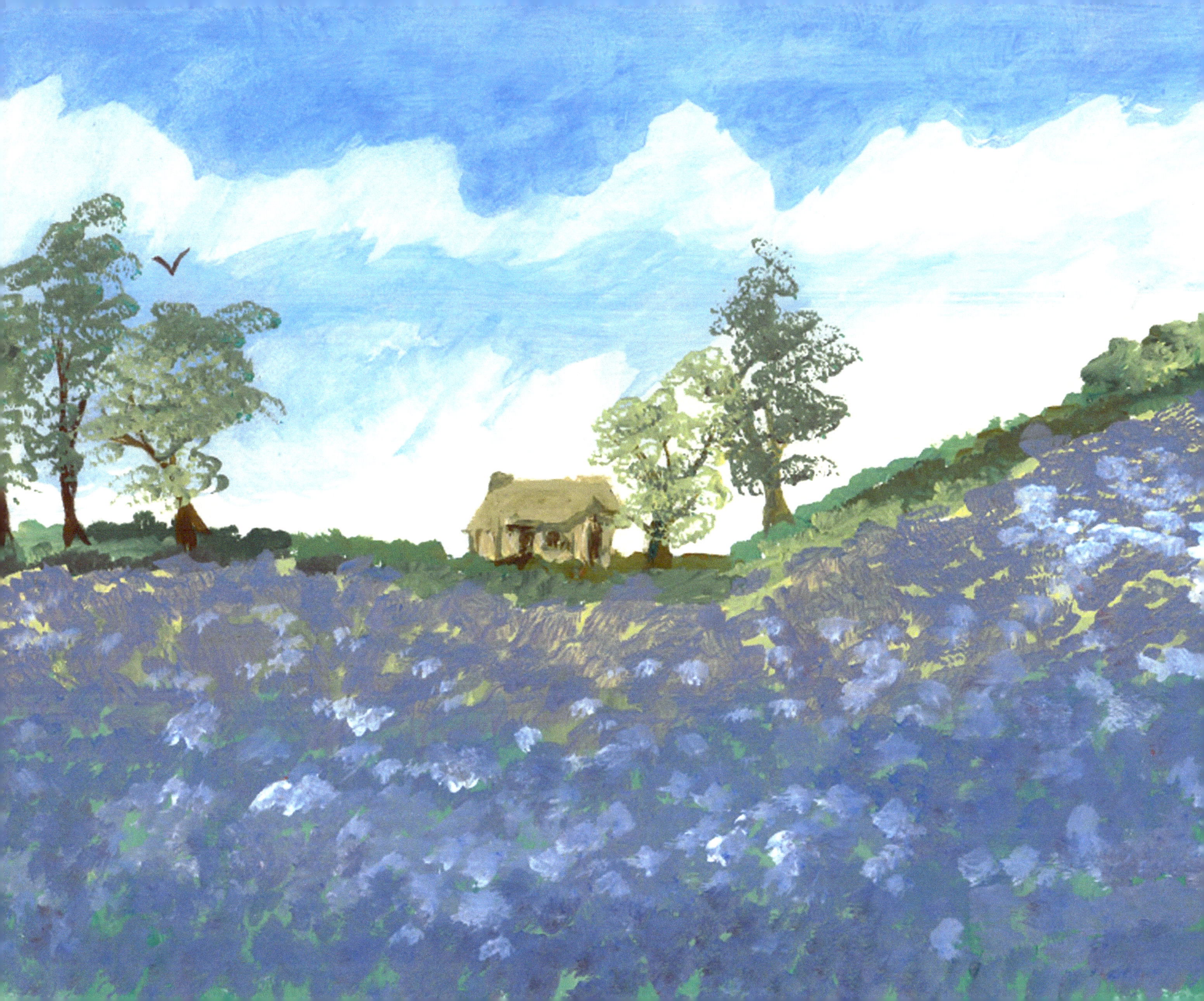

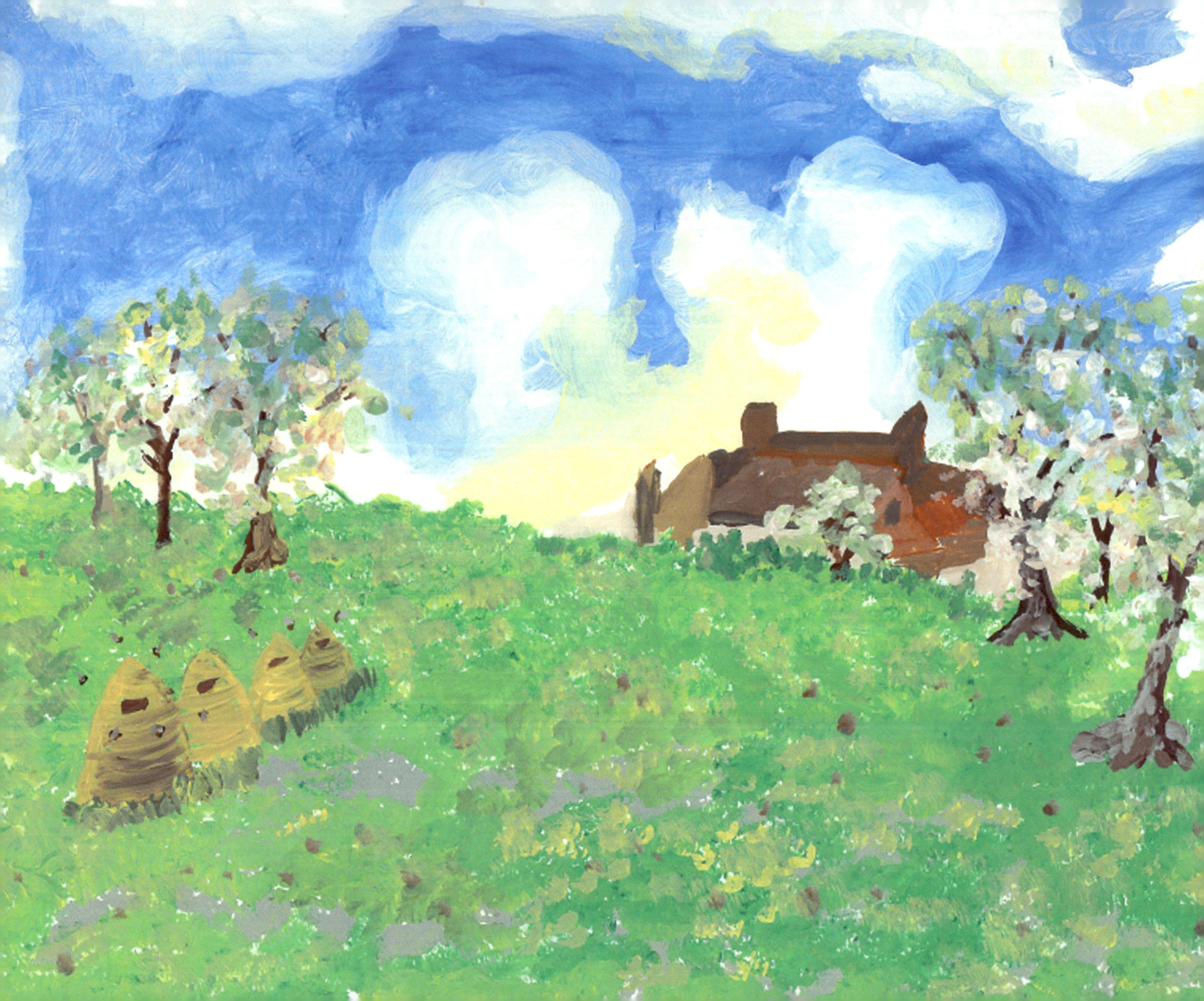

Tenant Farmers

"Whosoever sows sparingly shall also reap sparingly,
and whoever sows generously will also reap generously."
2 Corinthians 9:6

Serfdom had only come to an end in Prussia in 1806 with Napoleon's edict. It ended all personal bondage to landlords. Some farmers were able to buy their land by paying for it. They could pay for their land in installments. Some raised money by cutting down oak trees. Others worked farms as tenants. This may have been the case with my ancestors. The Prussian government only permitted one child to inherit the farm. The siblings were lent small parcels of land and stayed in a small house. Farmers paid a small rent and were required to work for the landowners on their farm as well. They could make a secondary income by working in cottage industries like processing hemp or flax to make rope or cloth.

Everyone on the farm was expected to work hard and to be productive. The women would be responsible for childcare, food preparation, spinning and weaving, gardening, and cleaning. Men would manage the construction of the home and onsite buildings, plowing, planting and harvesting crops, care for the livestock, chopping wood and bringing goods to market, and do offsite work for extra income. The children helped with cooking, gardening, milking, gathering eggs, and cleaning. The older ones would help with the cottage industry work.

The Auf-der-Haars were identified as being landowners. Keeping and managing a family farm is challenging work today. I imagine that the work then, with primitive tools and fewer resources, would have made for a long and full day. My ancestors may have been invested in the growing and processing of flax, bee keeping, keeping a home garden, and raising some livestock.

Provider and Protector

"He who works with his hands is a laborer. He who works with his hands and his head is a craftsman. He who works with his hands and his head, and his heart is an artist."
— Francis of Assisi

Johann Heinrich Wilhelm Auf-der-Haar was most likely a tenant farmer who worked at least 7–12 acres of land. He would have had long hours of labor in the field. This would have included plowing, sowing, and harvesting produce from the field, building and maintaining structures on the farm, chopping wood, caring for the livestock, and taking goods to the market for sale in Munster. As the husband, he was the head of the house. All financial business was decided by him. Child discipline after the age of 6 would also have been a duty.

The soil in Ladbergen was described as poor and sandy. This would have limited production, but most farmers were able to grow potatoes, cabbages, rye, buckwheat, beets, hemp, and flax. Staples like wheat, oats, sugar, spices, and oil would need to be purchased at the larger markets. Heinrich may have purchased these items in the nearby town of Munster.

In addition to farming and family responsibilities, men often practiced a trade or worked as a day laborer on someone else's plots. Trades included shoemaking, weaving, tailoring, baking, building wagons, masonry, carpentry, blacksmithing, and brewing. Shoemakers commonly made the affordable and functional wooden clogs. These remained popular footwear for this region till the mid 20th century.

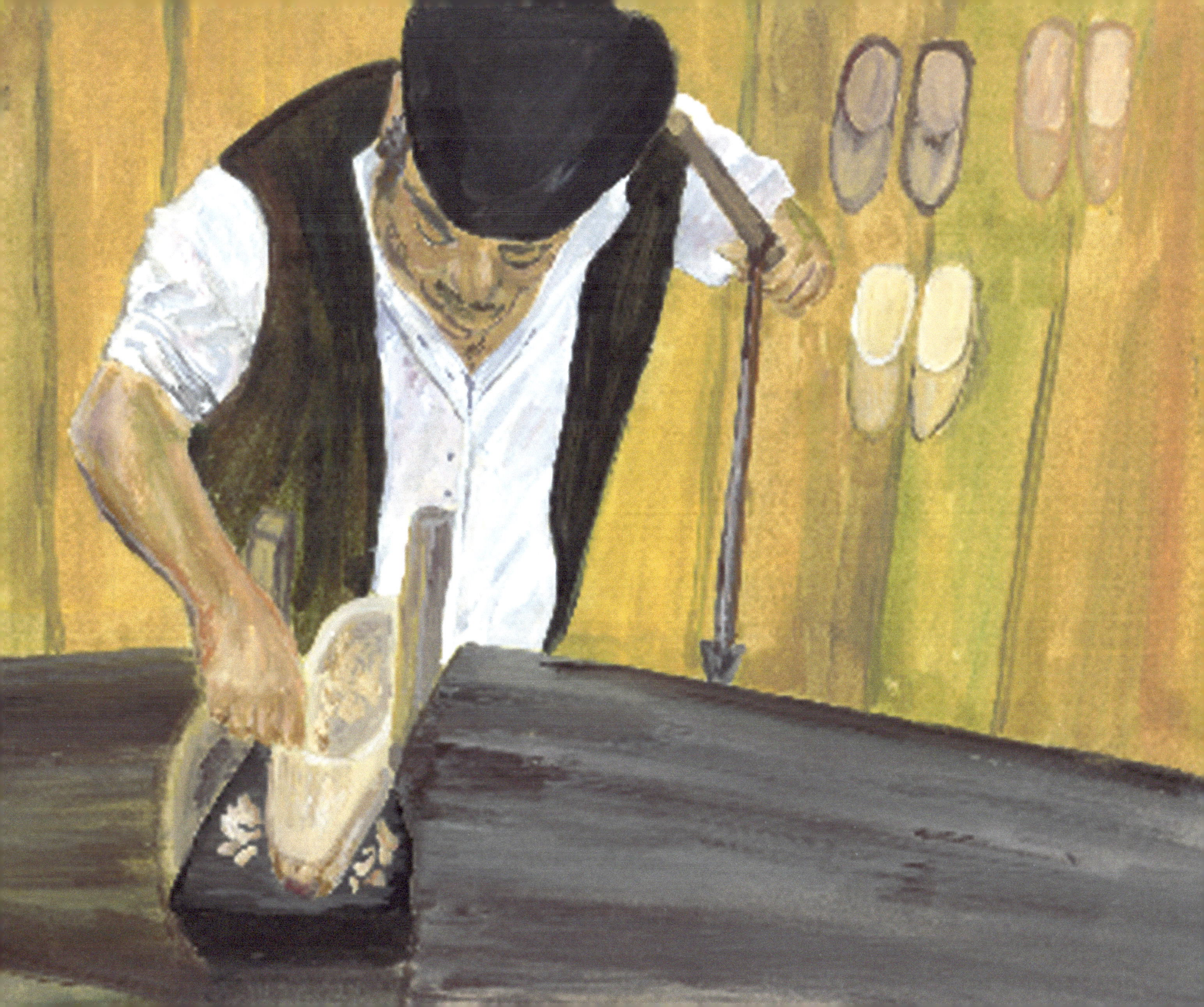

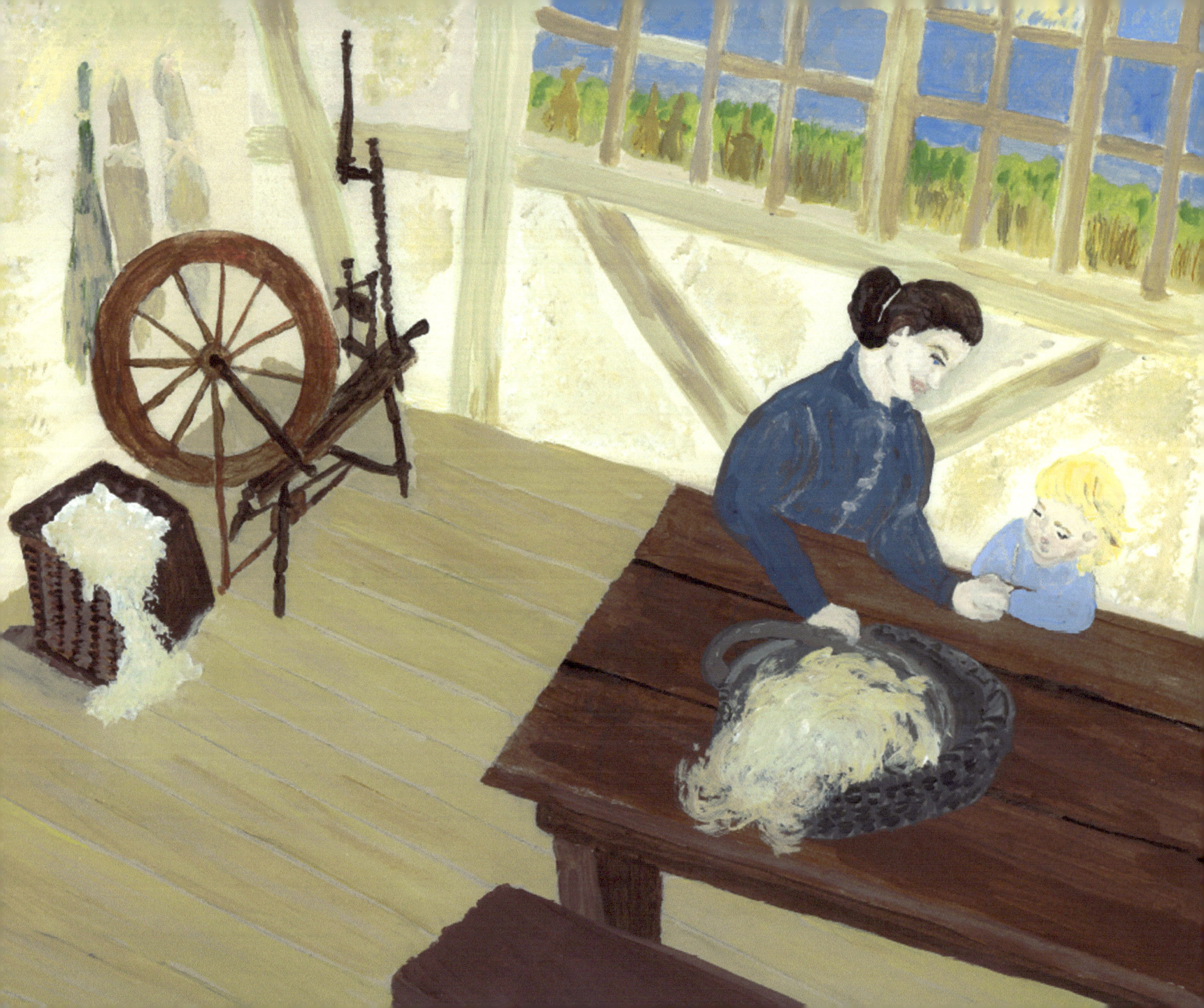

Homemaker and Caregiver

"She seeks wool and flax and works with willing hands."
PROVERBS 31:13

Christina Ann Elisabeth was just 29 but had three young children when they boarded the Leontine. Women married young and started families right away. During the childbearing years, most women had 5-7 successful pregnancies. Miscarriages and infant deaths were common. We don't know if Elisabeth experienced miscarriages.

To manage a farm household successfully, Elisabeth would have been hard at work from early morning to late in the evening. Her tasks would have included caring for the children, feeding the livestock, cooking meals over an open hearth, washing, sewing and mending clothes, cleaning, preserving food, tending the crops, harvesting, hauling water from the well, milking the cow, and baking. She may have also helped with processing flax and weaving linen as most homes were equipped with a spinning wheel and loom. Her time to rest would have been on Sundays, as church attendance was mandatory, and working on Sundays was frowned upon!

Children's Chores and Household Tales

"You people do not see that it is a straw the rooster is carrying and not a beam?"
— "The Rooster Beam," Jakob and Wilhelm Grimm

Wilhelm and Elisabeth would have been very busy on the farm. The baby, Christine, was still too young to help. They would have been asked to feed the chickens, collect the eggs, help with weeding, washing the clothes, and processing the flax. The children may have also helped with foraging for medicinal plants and foods like berries and mushrooms for food. Wilhelm would have attended the local village school to learn basic reading, writing, and arithmetic. Prussia was one of the first regions to require compulsory education for children aged 5–14. Daughters would have been traditionally taught by their mothers. But both children would have enjoyed hearing local folktales.

The concept of Kulturnation was a movement to strengthen the cultural and ethical identity of the German people. The Brothers Grimm, Jakob and Wilhelm, were integral to this movement. These civil servants, who were also scholars and researchers of local folklore, collected the fairytales that would create a common culture. Perhaps the two children imagined their rooster to be the magician's pet featured in the Grimm Fairytale, "The Rooster Beam." In the story, a young girl with a lucky four-leaf clover spots the deception of a traveling magician who is trying to deceive the villagers into believing that his rooster is incredibly strong. The girl can see that it is only straw the rooster carries and not a beam. Because of her integrity and courage, she can protect her neighbors from the magician's chicanery.

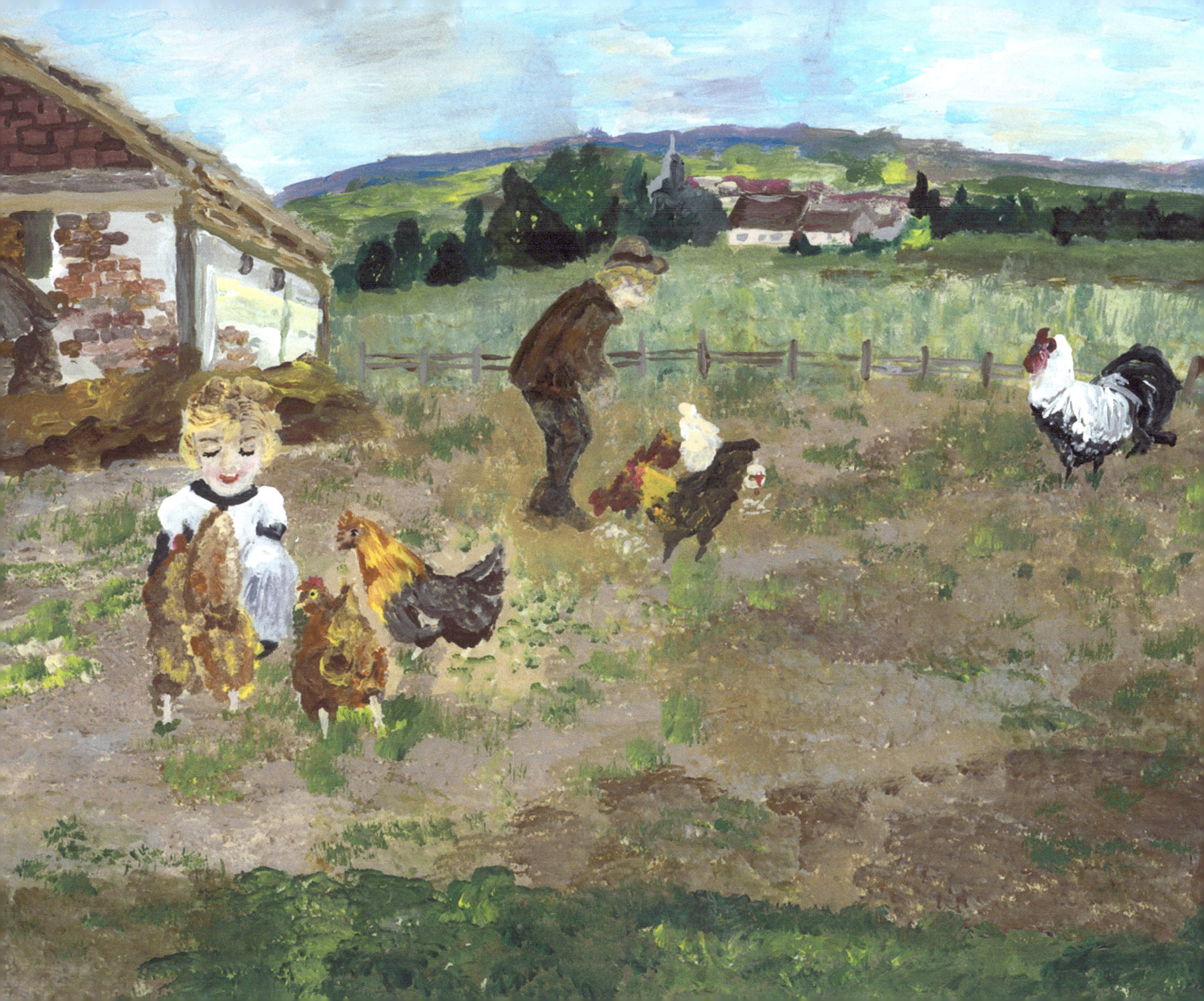

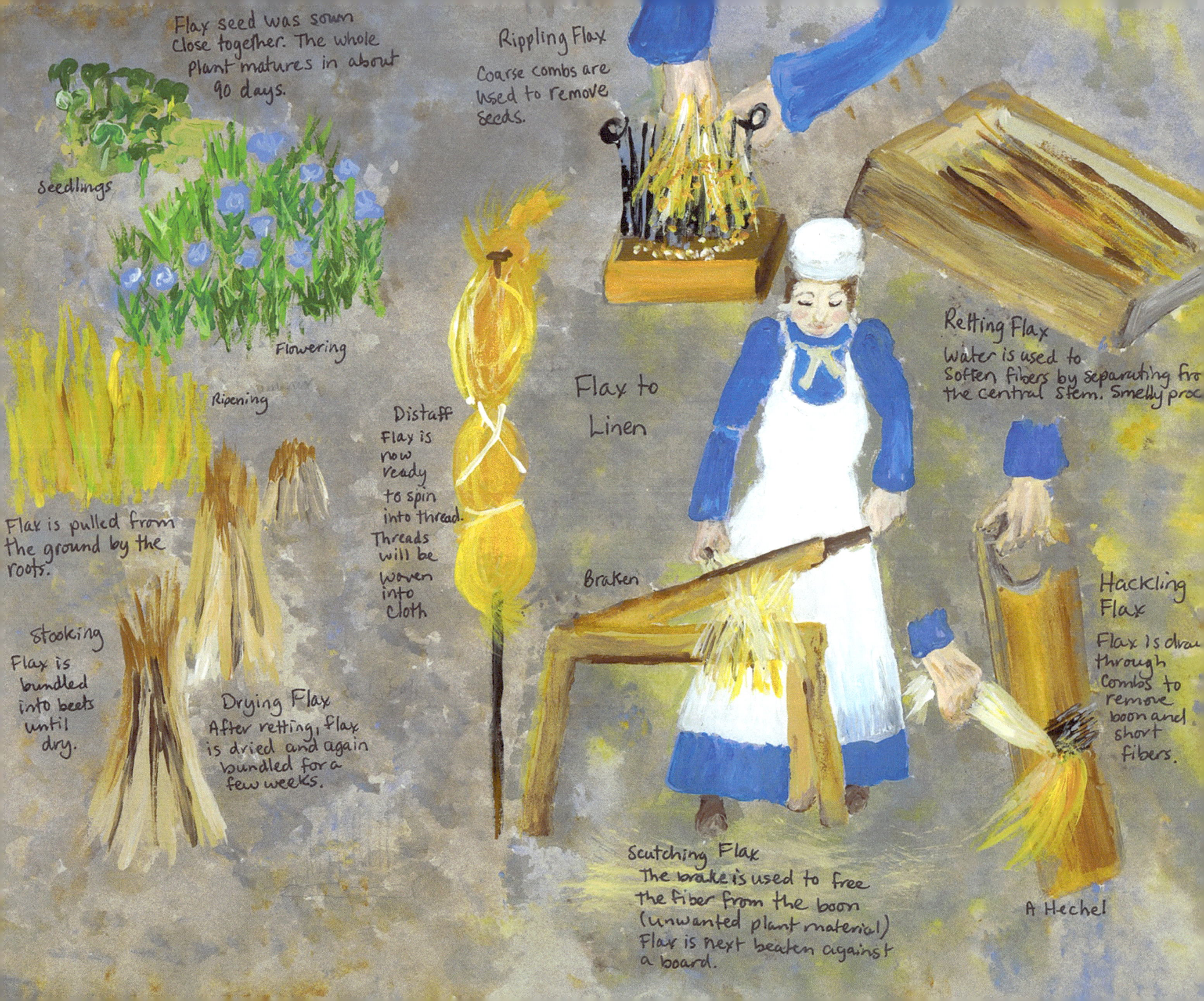
Flax seed was sown close together. The whole plant matures in about 90 days.
Seedlings
Flowering
Ripening
Flax is pulled from the ground by the roots.
Stooking
Flax is bundled into beets until dry.
Drying Flax
After retting, flax is dried and again bundled for a few weeks.
Distaff
Flax is now ready to spin into thread. Threads will be woven into cloth
Flax to Linen
Rippling Flax
Coarse combs are used to remove seeds.
Retting Flax
Water is used to soften fibers by separating fro the central stem. Smelly proc
Braken
Hackling Flax
Flax is drau through combs to remove boon and short fibers.
A Hechel
Scutching Flax
The brake is used to free the fiber from the boon (unwanted plant material) Flax is next beaten against a board.

A Prosperous Cottage Industry
Flax to Linen

"Man works til set of sun; Woman's work is never done.
From rise of morn to set of sun, Woman's work is never done."
— Proverb

Flax and hemp were both grown for their use in woven goods, edible seeds, and oils. The cottage industry of linen production provided a steady income for farm families up until the continental blockade by Napoleon in 1807. This caused it to gradually decline as a major source of wealth.

Fields of flax were sown in the spring and harvested three months later in the early fall. Flax would be pulled by the roots during harvesting for the fibers to be long. Pulling was hard work, and back injuries were common. Flax was next bundled and tied into what were called beets. These were left to dry. This was called stooking.

To deseed the flax, the top ends of the dry bundles were pulled through a comb of nails. This was called rippling. Seeds were saved. During the retting process, the flax was soaked in ponds or troughs of water. This freed the fibers from the stalk. It was a very smelly process.

Next, the fibers were further softened by breaking the inner woody stalk into smaller pieces, thus separating the flax. These woody fragments were called shives. Remaining shives would be scutched out with a knife.

During Hackling, the flax was prepared for spinning by pulling it through nails. Fibers were held steady on a distaff, ready to be spun into yarn. This yarn would be woven into fabric and then bleached in the sun. Finally, it would be dyed and ready for use.

Beekeeping

*"One can no more approach people without love than one can approach bees without care.
Such is the quality of bees..."*
— Leo Tolstoy

On the Ladbergen crest, there are two bees. They symbolize the tax money that was once brought to the Freckenhorst monastery. Beekeeping had been common to the region since the 4th century. Flowers of the heath, flax, buckwheat, and apple blossoms would have provided nectar for the bees. Hemp was a good source of pollen.

Hives were made from weaving wicker, straw, and reed into circular structures called skeps. They were kept in a Bienenzaun, which was a bee enclosure resembling a shed. The skeps could be moved to common lands that provided sufficient forage and to allow pollination services.

Beeswax was important for making candles, and the honey was used as a sweetener and for making mead. Comb honey was a favorite luxury. Honey was also a key ingredient in baked goods, like Lebkuchen and honey cookies. Honey was also prized for its health qualities.

Black German bees, or the European dark bees, are somewhat aggressive but considered hardworking and productive. They are more prone to mites and more likely to swarm. It is for some of these reasons that they are now an endangered species.

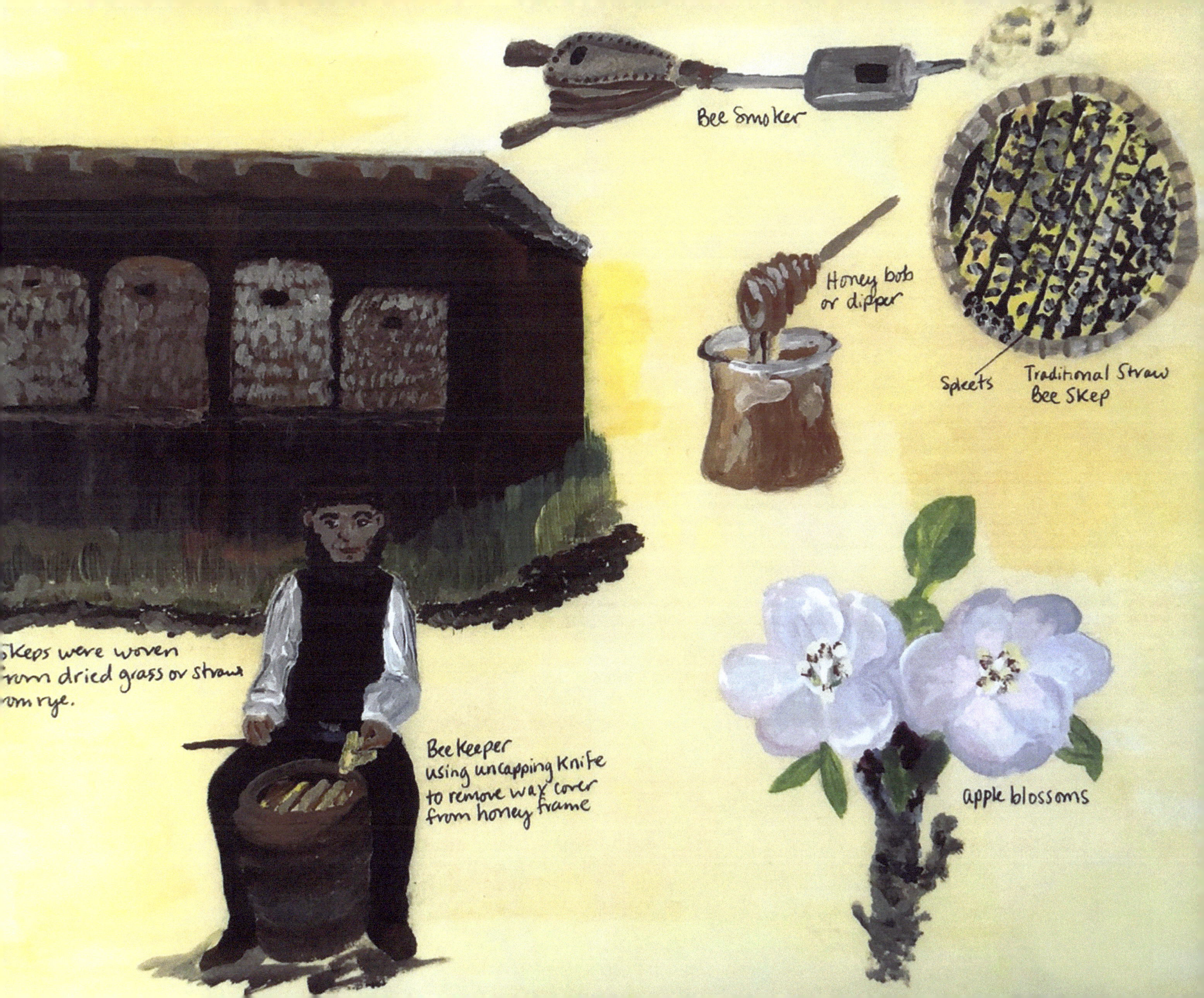
Bee Smoker
Honey bob or dipper
Spleets
Traditional Straw Bee Skep
Skeps were woven
rom dried grass or straw
om rye.
Bee Keeper
using uncapping Knife
to remove wax cover
from honey frame
apple blossoms

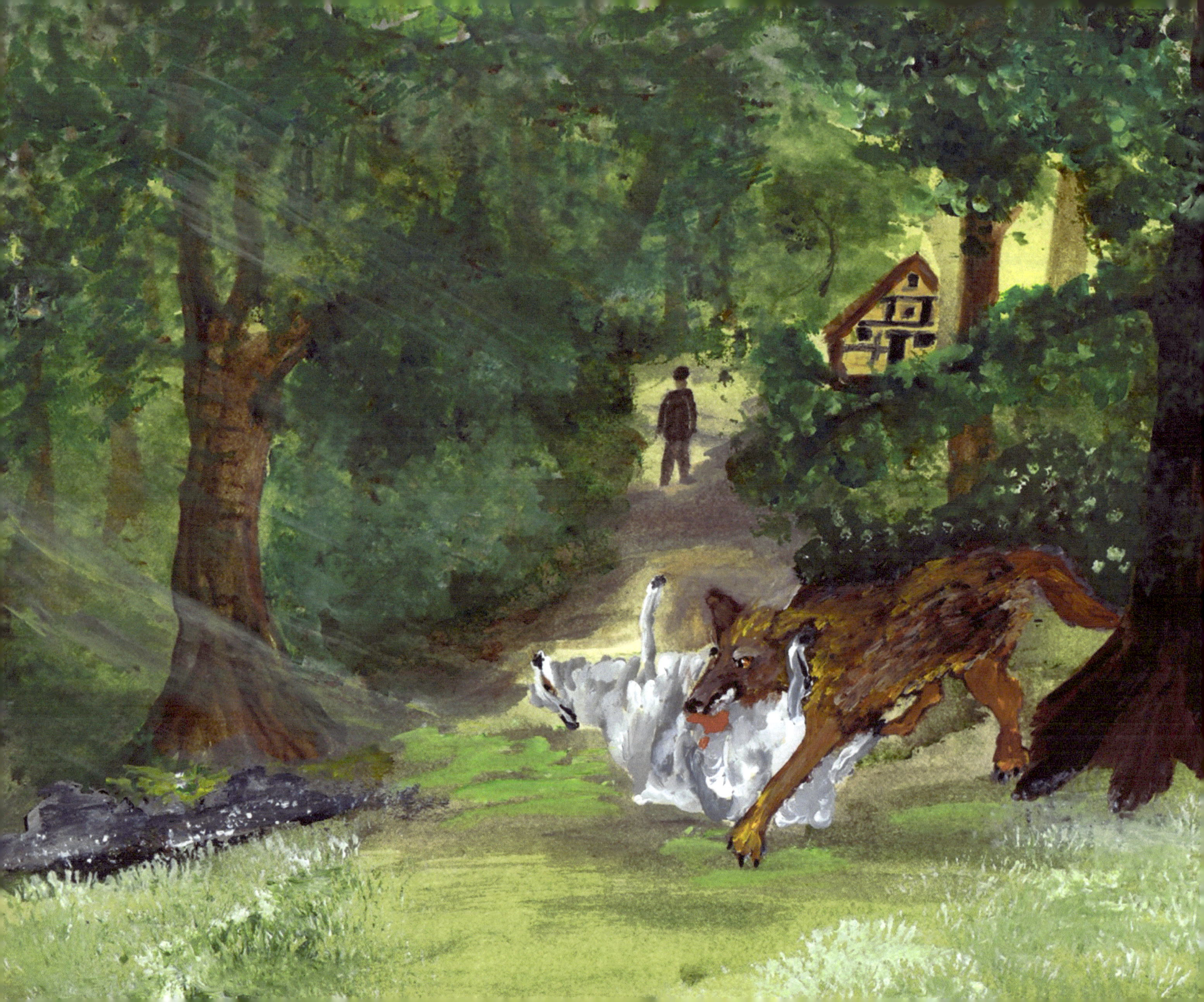

Protecting Home and Flock

"The painter should not paint what he sees, but what will be seen."
— Caspar David Friedrich

Life in a small village was not without its dangers. Due to the economic hardships of the times, theft had become more common. Roving bands of thieves would burglar homes and farms in Ladbergen and neighboring communities. Thefts of drying linen, food, and clothing were recorded. Punishment and retribution for thieving, however, was severe. If caught in the act, robbers could be beaten or even killed by villagers defending their property.

Wolves from the bordering heaths and marsh areas were also a threat to farmers and their livestock. Sheep were their favorite prey, but they had been known to attack people as well. One poor farmer was chased up a pine tree by wolves. Fortunately, his guard dogs protected him, although they were killed in the fight.

Military Service

"To secure peace is to prepare for war."
— Carl von Clausewitz, student of Scharnhorst

Village families hated conscription and compulsory military service. During the years under Napoleonic rule, single young men were pressed into service, and villagers were forced to quarter soldiers in their homes. The citizen soldier had a duty to bear arms in defense of the Kingdom of Prussia. Conscription created a source of trained recruits that would be ready for action. Many young men sought marriage to escape service. During the Russian campaign of 1812, the unlucky Ladbergens that were forced to join never returned. Under the strong leadership of the first Chief of the Prussian General Staff, Gerhard von Scharnhorst, the army developed new methods of organization, supply, mobility, and command. This restructuring gave the Prussian army the capability to aid their allies in the defeat and expulsion of Napoleon during the Wars of Liberation 1813-1814. Having a strong army would later allow Prussia to unify Germany and to establish the German Empire in 1871.

Scharnhorst was instrumental in creating the system of universal service. Single men between the ages of 17-25 were subject to military draft for three years. Men of these ages were forbidden to emigrate. Some young men still left the country secretly and escaped to America. For many young men, their loyalties were to their faith and family and not to fighting in wars.

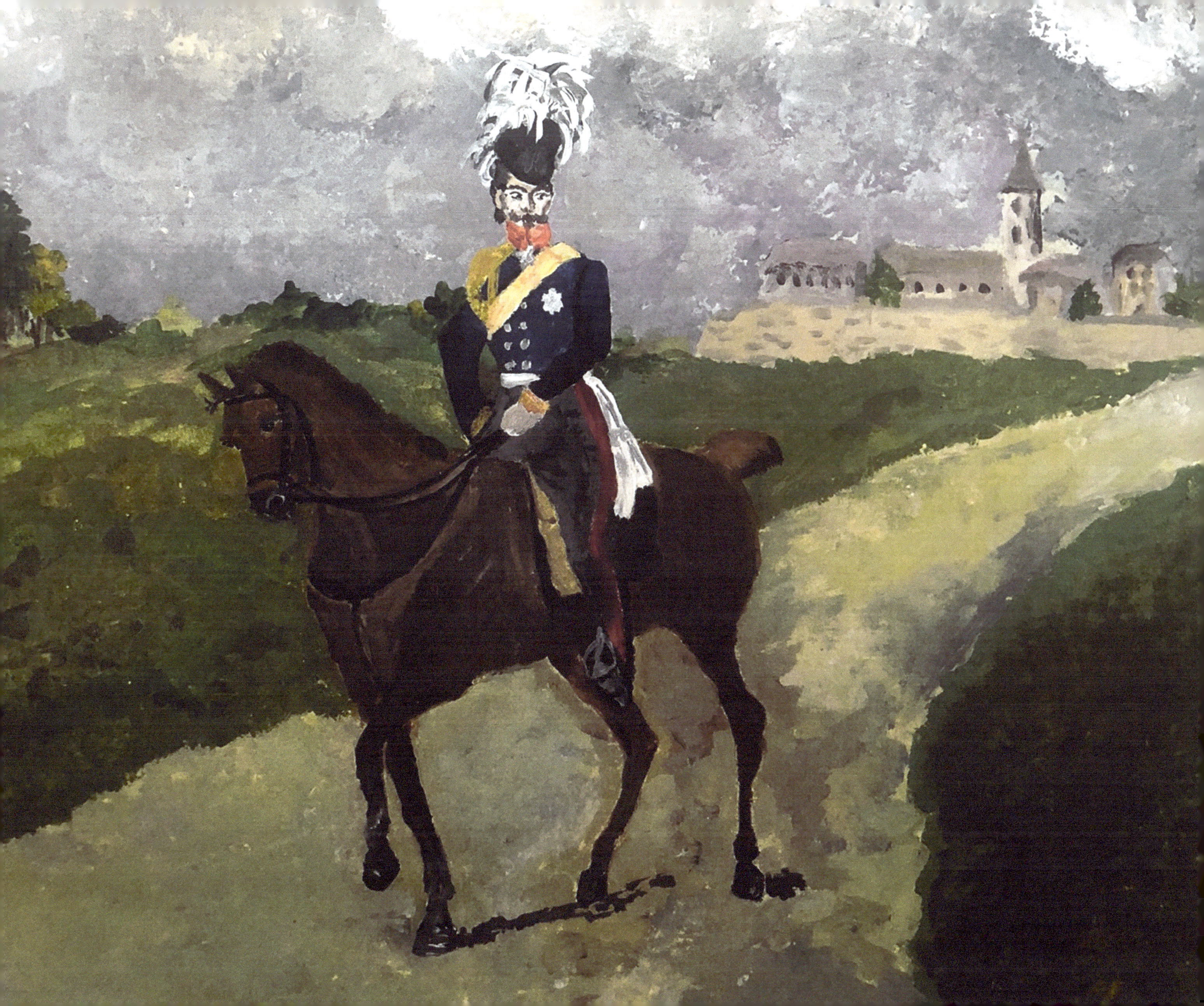

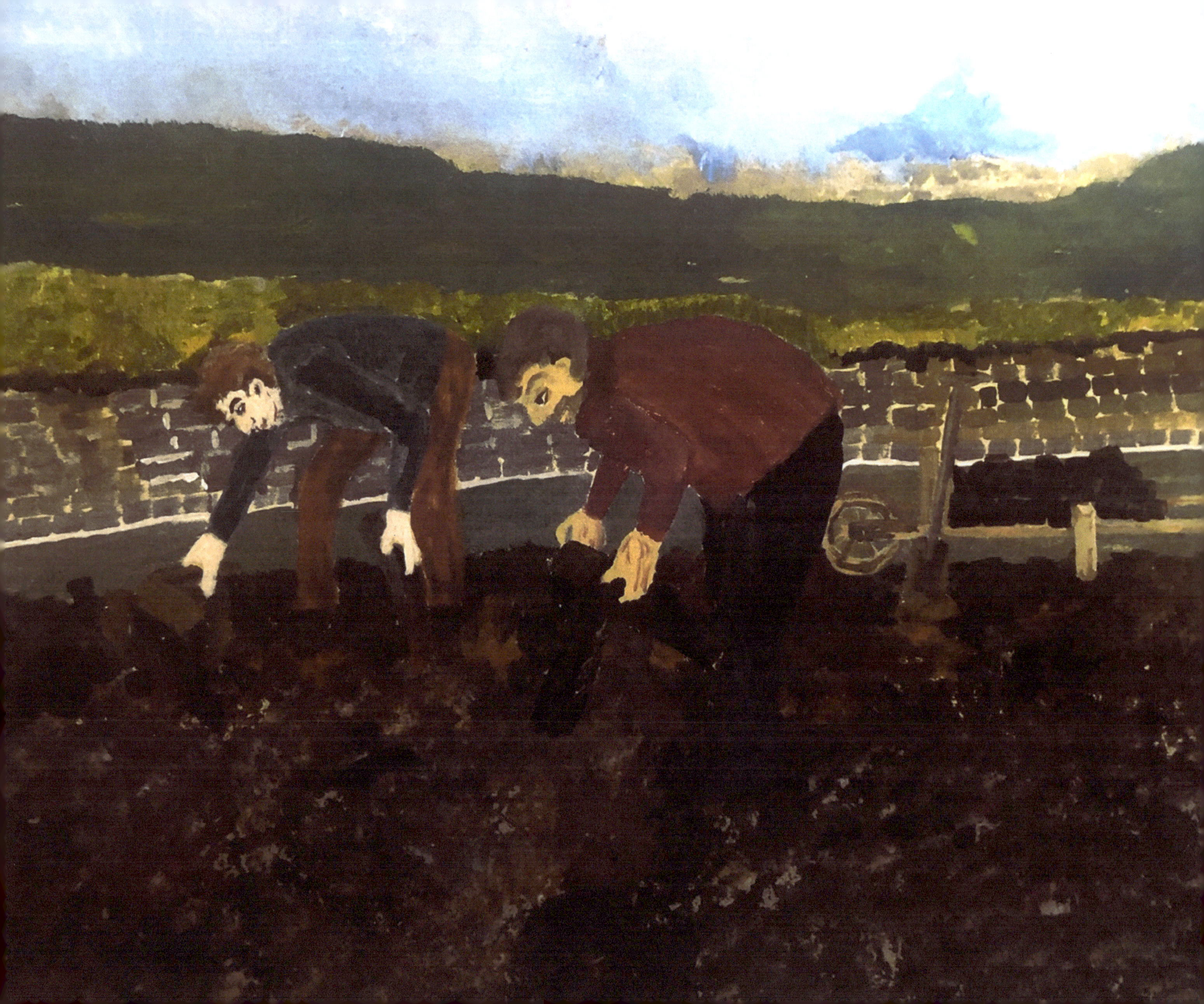

Work in the Peat Bogs

"This is the mark of a really admirable man: steadfastness in the face of trouble."
— Ludwig van Beethoven

At one time, Ladbergen had many swampy areas where peat moss could be removed. Peat moss was used as a fuel source for domestic fires and as an antiseptic bandage for wounds. The sphagnum moss dressing was highly absorbent and created a sterile environment for healing.

As a fuel source, it would be cut into bricks and stacked to dry. Peat was much cheaper than coal and easier to access. Men from Ladbergen would seek migrant work in Holland near Dedemsvaart during the spring and summer months to cut and move peat. It was laborious and unhealthy work that required them to stand in water while cutting the peat. They made temporary shelters from sod for their homes. Workers suffered from arthritis, pneumonia, and other diseases. Strikes were common due to poor wages and living conditions.

Migrant work in Holland did subsidize their incomes and made survival for poor farming families possible. Other seasonal work in Holland included cutting grass, threshing, construction, and working as sailors on whaling ships. My ancestors were hardworking and able to endure much hardship to provide for their families.

Faith and the Church

"Thou Lamb of God, Thou Prince of Peace,
For Thee my thirsty soul doth pine.
My longing heart implores Thy grace.
O make me in Thy likeness shine!"
— Christian Friedrich Richter

The Auf-der-Haars were members of the Reformed Church, or the Evangelical Church, in Westphalia. Their church was originally built in the 14th century. The church was enlarged in 1756 but damaged by lightning in the 1800s. The tower was removed in the 1830s, and in 1854, the old church was torn down. Pastor Gustav Lenhartz would oversee the building of the new church. All landowners paid taxes to the church, the pastor, and the organist. Taxes were often in the form of agricultural products like honey, grain, or livestock. Church attendance was mandatory and failure to attend could result in discipline.

The Protestants of this region were very conservative in their views and were not tolerant of proponents of the Enlightenment. Life in Ladbergen was challenging and often cut short by disease. Life expectancy for most was 40–50 years old. So, hope was placed more in securing an afterlife in heaven rather than in wealth and comfort in the present world. The Heidelberg Catechism of 1563 was still used to train children in their religious lessons. The parishioners would have enjoyed a scripted sermon from the pastor and would have engaged in singing traditional hymns accompanied by the organist.

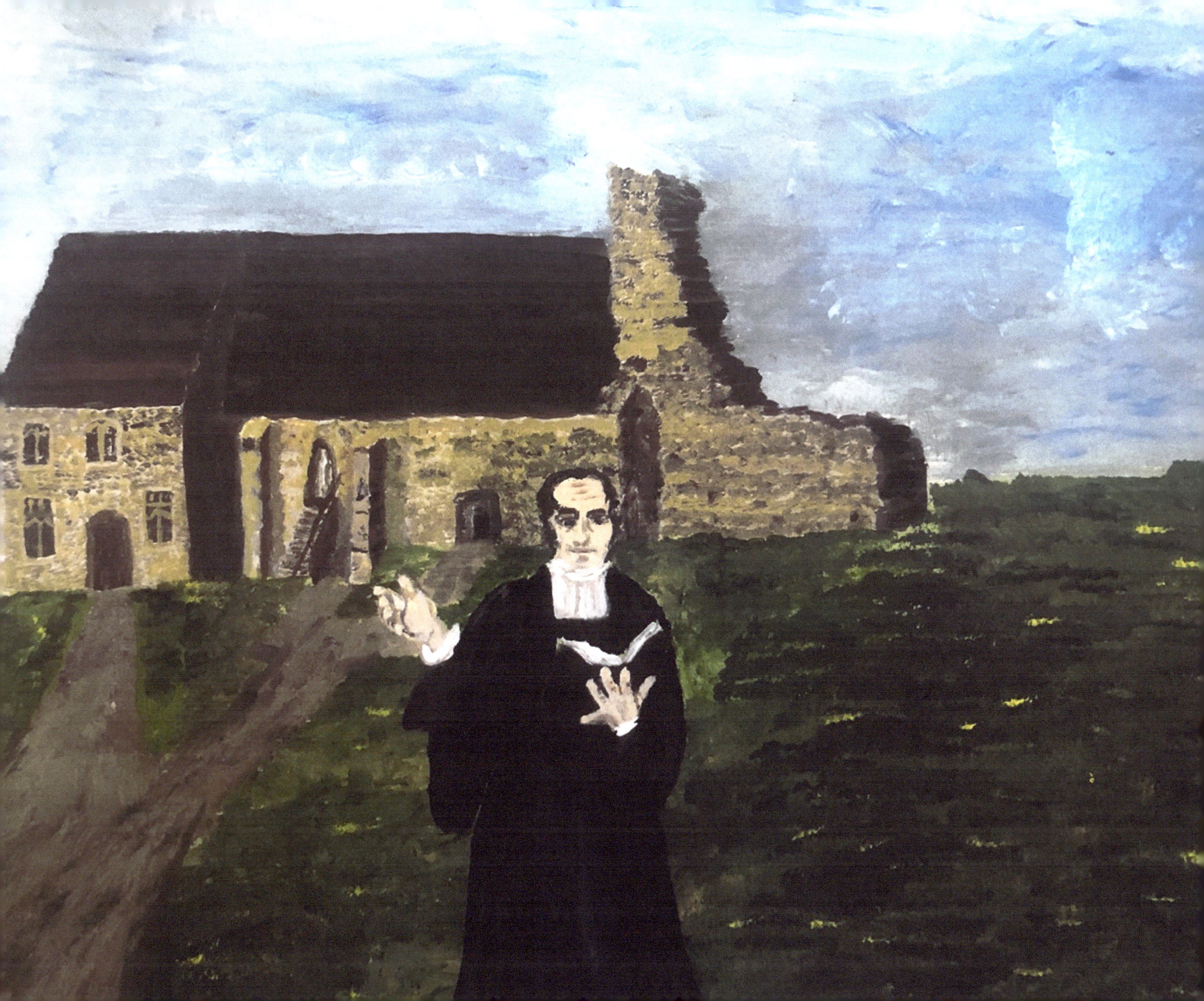

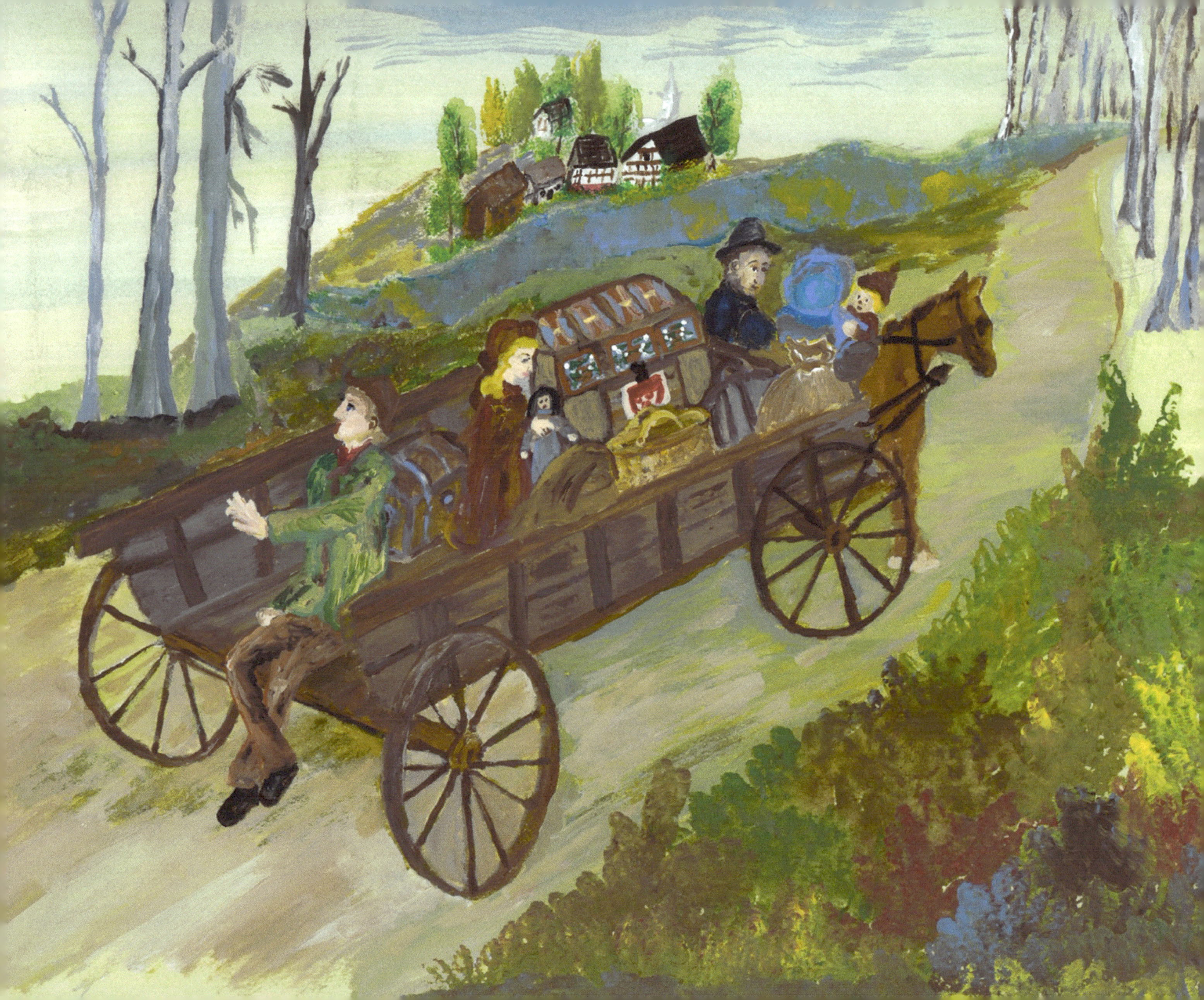

Moving Day

"The length of the journey has to be borne with, for every moment is necessary."
— Georg Wilhelm Friedrich Hegel

Saying goodbye to friends, family, and your homeland must have been a challenging time. The Auf-der-Haars and Feigenbaums had lived in the region for generations, but continued economic hardships were forcing them to leave. The market for flax and weaving of linen for export had dried up. Privatization of the common lands for pasturing animals and foraging was a huge loss that could not be overcome. The fear of having their sons drafted into the military was another real concern.

Some families had already made the move to America, and their letters were full of hope and promise. Land in the Midwest was affordable and help from these new settlers would make the move possible. Traveling to a new land and culture is not as frightening when you know that some of your kin and friends have already settled and are successfully farming. They would travel with their heritage of farming, weaving, food preservation, and Protestant faith. A farmer and a carpenter that had survived in the worst of times would have the grit and resourcefulness to survive in their new home in America.

Across the Big Pond

*"Ah, how uplifting it is to delight
in the infinity of the ocean!
There is no longer any thought of size and space
concealed as a goal for our dreams."*
— Restlessness, Annette von Droste-Hulshoff

Our Heinrich H. Aufderhaar left his homeland of Ladbergen, Germany in 1847. He was 15 when he arrived in the USA. He married Mary Elisabeth Auf-der-Haar in 1866. She was the daughter of Johann Heinrich Wilhem Auf-Der-Haar and Anna Elisabeth Fiegenbaum. There are quite a few similarities with names as descendants were often given similar family names as a way of keeping that person's memory alive. Names were also sometimes changed or even dropped when coming to America. We do know that our ancestors are from Ladbergen and that they came to the USA during the big emigration period from 1830 to 1850. Chain migration, where friends, family, and cultural institutions helped fellow immigrants find their way in America, was a highly successful network. Our ancestors would make their home west of St. Louis, Missouri. We also have distant cousins in New Knoxville, Ohio as a large population of emigrants from Ladbergen settled there.

The land in the mid-western states was excellent for farming and was mostly flat like the home they had left. The transition to the states would not have been too overwhelming as they brought much of their culture and traditions with them. They had found their sense of space, die Landschaften, and had made it into their home.

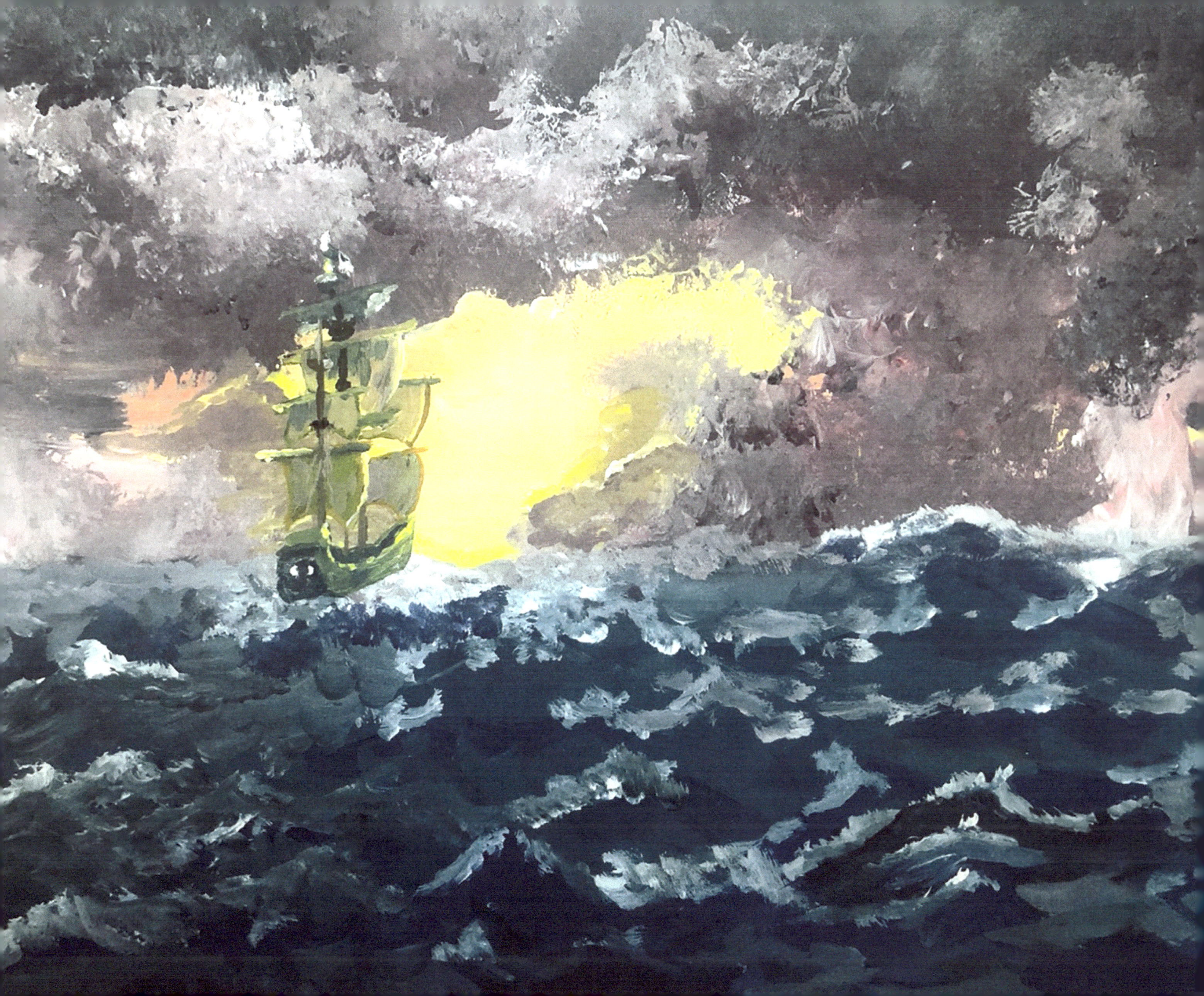

Apfelpfannkuchen or Pfannkuchen
– German Apple Pancake

The Americanized version is also called a Bismarck, a Dutch puff, a Dutch baby or a Hootenanny. It is an apple and egg dish similar to a popover since it is leavened by steam.

Ingredients
- ¼ c. butter
- ¼ c. sugar (beet sugar or brown sugar)
- 1 tsp. cinnamon
- ½ tsp. nutmeg
- ⅛ tsp. cloves
- 2 tart apples, peeled and sliced thin

- 3 eggs
- ½ c. whole milk
- 1 tsp. vanilla
- ½ c. all-purpose flour
- ¼ tsp. kosher or sea salt

Whisk made from the Downy birch tree

Antique Nutmeg grater

Alte Apfelsorten
Old Apple varieties

Altländer Pfannkuchenapfel
Old country Pancake apple

Weißer Klarapfel
White Transparent

Directions   Yield: 4-6

1. Preheat oven to 425°F.
2. Melt butter in cast iron skillet. Add sugar and spices. Toss with apples to coat. Remove from heat.
3. In a bowl, beat together the eggs, milk, and vanilla. Sift in flour and salt. Whisk to combine.
4. Pour batter over the apple mixture.
5. Bake in oven for 20 minutes.
6. Allow to cool for four minutes, before slicing into generous wedges.
7. Serve with powdered sugar, heated syrups and or fresh fruit.

Optional – add in cooked bacon or sausage.

Apfelpfannkuchen or Pfannkuchen
German Apple Pancake

Yield: 4–6 servings

Ingredients

¼ cup butter

¼ cup sugar (beet sugar or brown sugar)

1 tsp. cinnamon

½ tsp. nutmeg

⅛ tsp. cloves

2 tart apples, peeled and sliced thin

***

3 eggs

½ cup whole milk

1 tsp. vanilla

½ cup all-purpose flour

¼ tsp. Kosher or sea salt

Directions

1. Preheat oven to 425°F.
2. Melt butter in cast iron skillet. Add sugar and spices. Toss with apples to coat. Remove from heat.
3. In a bowl, beat together the eggs, milk, and vanilla. Sift in flour and salt. Whisk to combine.
4. Pour batter over the apple mixture.
5. Bake in oven for 20 minutes.
6. Allow to cool for four minutes, before slicing into generous wedges.
7. Serve with powdered sugar, heated syrups, and/or fresh fruit.

Optional: add in cooked bacon or sausage.

About the Author

Ancestral Travels is the product of family research and hobbies of a retired high school teacher. Joye Cantrell is a graduate of Appalachian State University and California State University of San Bernardino. Joye holds teaching degrees in home economics and science. She had the pleasure of teaching culinary arts and environmental science students in Rialto, California for 30 years. Joye also taught in Georgia and North Carolina. Her hobbies include cooking, painting, woodworking, and road tripping with her husband, Steven Cantrell, and their fur baby, Mimi.

Bibliography

Brooks, Arthur. "Our Family Story." Genealogical Research. 2011.

Citino, Robert M. *The German Way of War: From the Thirty Years' War to the Third Reich*. University Press of Kansas, 2005.

Fiegenbaum Family Website. "The Bark Leontine from Bremen To Baltimore" Passenger List at Baltimore, Maryland on 28 June 1841., http://www.fiegenbaum.org/genealogy/migration/leontine1841.htm. Accessed 23 Oct. 2023.

"Flax to Linen: How to Grow Flaxseed and Transform It into Linen Cloth." *YouTube*, YouTube, 26 Feb. 2021, www.youtube.com/watch

Frost, Helen. *German Immigrants, 1820-1920*. Blue Earth Books, 2002.

Hoge, Dean R., and Willi Untiet. *From Ladbergen to America: The Heritage and the Migration*. New Knoxville Historical Society, 2007.

Kruger, Anne Sturm. *Growing Up at Emmaus 1910-1938*. Family Heritage Publishers, 2022.

Museum Display. New Knoxville Historical Society, New Knoxville, OH.

Rippley, Lavern. *Of German Ways*. Dillon Pr, 1973.

Saatkamp, Friedrich, and Dean R. Hoge. *Ladbergen: Out of the History and the Present of the 1000-Year Westphalian Village*. New Knoxville Historical Society, 1985.

Scheer, Teva J. *Our Daily Bread: Village Life in Early Modern Germany*. Adventis Press, 2010.

Seymour, John. *Forgotten Household Crafts*. Dorling Kindersley, 2007.

Sturm, William Paul. "*Sturm Genealogy*." File Cabinet Notes. 2018.

www.ingramcontent.com/pod-product-compliance
Lightning Source LLC
Chambersburg PA
CBHW041951150426

43196CB00004B/59